W9-CIC-036

Your Government:
How It Works

The Vice Presidency

Marilyn D. Anderson

Arthur M. Schlesinger, jr.
Senior Consulting Editor

Chelsea House Publishers
Philadelphia

CHELSEA HOUSE PUBLISHERS
Production Manager Pamela Loos
Art Director Sara Davis
Director of Photography Judy L. Hasday
Managing Editor James D. Gallagher
Senior Production Editor J. Christopher Higgins

Staff for THE VICE PRESIDENCY
Project Editor/Publishing Coordinator Jim McAvoy
Associate Art Director Takeshi Takahashi
Series Designers Takeshi Takahashi, Keith Trego

First Printing
1 3 5 7 9 8 6 4 2

Library of Congress Cataloging-in-Publication Data

Anderson, Marilyn D.
  The Vice Presidency / Marilyn D. Anderson.
    p. cm. — (Your government—how it works)
  Includes bibliographical references and index.
  ISBN 0-7910-5997-9
  1. Vice-Presidents—United States—Juvenile literature.
[1. Vice-Presidents.] I. Title. II. Series.

JK609.5 .A666 2000
973'.09'9—dc21   00-034587

Contents

YOUR GOVERNMENT
HOW IT WORKS

The Attorney General's Office

The Cabinet

The Central Intelligence Agency

The Drug Enforcement Administration

The Federal Bureau of Investigation

The History of the Democratic Party

The History of the Republican Party

The History of Third Parties

The House of Representatives

How a Bill Is Passed

How to Become an Elected Official

The Impeachment Process

The Internal Revenue Service

The Presidency

The Secretary of State

The Senate

The Speaker of the House of Representatives

The Supreme Court

The U.S. Armed Forces

The U.S. Constitution

The U.S. Secret Service

The Vice Presidency

Introduction

Government: Crises of Confidence

Arthur M. Schlesinger, jr.

FROM THE START, Americans have regarded their government with a mixture of reliance and mistrust. The men who founded the republic understood the importance of government. "If men were angels," observed the 51st Federalist Paper, "no government would be necessary." But men are not angels. Because human beings are subject to wicked as well as to noble impulses, government was deemed essential to assure freedom and order.

The American revolutionaries, however, also knew that government could become a source of injury and oppression. The men who gathered in Philadelphia in 1787 to write the Constitution therefore had two purposes in mind: They wanted to establish a strong central authority and to limit that central authority's capacity to abuse its power.

To prevent the abuse of power, the Founding Fathers wrote two basic principles into the Constitution. The principle of federalism divided power between the state governments and the central authority. The principle of the separation of powers subdivided the central authority itself into three branches—the executive, the legislative, and the judiciary—so that "each may be a check on the other."

YOUR GOVERNMENT: HOW IT WORKS examines some of the major parts of that central authority, the federal government. It explains how various officials, agencies, and departments operate and explores the political organizations that have grown up to serve the needs of government.

Introduction

The federal government as presented in the Constitution was more an idealistic construct than a practical administrative structure. It was barely functional when it came into being.

This was especially true of the executive branch. The Constitution did not describe the executive branch in any detail. After vesting executive power in the president, it assumed the existence of "executive departments" without specifying what these departments should be. Congress began defining their functions in 1789 by creating the Departments of State, Treasury, and War.

President Washington, assisted by Secretary of the Treasury Alexander Hamilton, equipped the infant republic with a working administrative structure. Congress also continued that process by creating more executive departments as they were needed.

Throughout the 19th century, the number of federal government workers increased at a consistently faster rate than did the population. Increasing concerns about the politicization of public service led to efforts—bitterly opposed by politicians—to reform it in the latter part of the century.

The 20th century saw considerable expansion of the federal establishment. More importantly, it saw growing impatience with bureaucracy in society as a whole.

The Great Depression during the 1930s confronted the nation with its greatest crisis since the Civil War. Under Franklin Roosevelt, the New Deal reshaped the federal government, assigning it a variety of new responsibilities and greatly expanding its regulatory functions. By 1940, the number of federal workers passed the 1 million mark.

Critics complained of big government and bureaucracy. Business owners resented federal regulation. Conservatives worried about the impact of paternalistic government on self-reliance, on community responsibility, and on economic and personal freedom.

When the United States entered World War II in 1941, government agencies focused their energies on supporting the war effort. By the end of World War II, federal civilian employment had risen to 3.8 million. With peace, the federal establishment declined to around 2 million in 1950. Then growth resumed, reaching 2.8 million by the 1980s.

A large part of this growth was the result of the national government assuming new functions such as: affirmative action in civil rights, environmental protection, and safety and health in the workplace.

Some critics became convinced that the national government was a steadily growing behemoth swallowing up the liberties of the people. The 1980s brought new intensity to the debate about government growth. Foes of Washington bureaucrats preferred local government, feeling it more responsive to popular needs.

But local government is characteristically the government of the locally powerful. Historically, the locally powerless have often won their human and constitutional rights by appealing to the national government. The national government has defended racial justice against local bigotry, upheld the Bill of Rights against local vigilantism, and protected natural resources from local greed. It has civilized industry and secured the rights of labor organizations. Had the states' rights creed prevailed, perhaps slavery would still exist in the United States.

Americans are still of two minds. When pollsters ask large, spacious questions—Do you think government has become too involved in your lives? Do you think government should stop regulating business?—a sizable majority opposes big government. But when asked specific questions about the practical work of government—Do you favor Social Security? Unemployment compensation? Medicare? Health and safety standards in factories? Environmental protection?—a sizable majority approves of intervention.

We do not like bureaucracy, but we cannot live without it. We need its genius for organizing the intricate details of our daily lives. Without bureaucracy, modern society would collapse. It would be impossible to run any of the large public and private organizations we depend on without bureaucracy's division of labor and hierarchy of authority. The challenge is to keep these necessary structures of our civilization flexible, efficient, and capable of innovation.

More than 200 years after the drafting of the Constitution, Americans still rely on government but also mistrust it. These attitudes continue to serve us well. What we mistrust, we are more likely to monitor. And government needs our constant attention if it is to avoid inefficiency, incompetence, and arbitrariness. Without our informed participation, it cannot serve us individually or help us as a people to attain the lofty goals of the Founding Fathers.

A Secret Service agent climbs into the back of President Kennedy's limousine as it rushes to a hospital. Lyndon B. Johnson assumed the responsibilities of the presidency when Kennedy was pronounced dead at Dallas Parkland Hospital.

CHAPTER

Facing a Tragedy: November 1963

AT ABOUT 12:30 P.M. ON NOVEMBER 22, 1963, a shot was fired from a mail-order rifle. It sent the United States of America into a tail-spin. Newscasters emotionally declared: "The president has been shot!"

About an hour earlier Vice President Lyndon Johnson's plane, *Air Force Two*, had landed in Dallas, Texas. He and his wife, Lady Bird Johnson, were cheered as they stepped from the plane in their home state. Minutes later President John F. Kennedy and his wife arrived on *Air Force One*.

Soon the president, Mrs. Kennedy, Governor John Connelly of Texas, and the governor's wife got into the first of a string of open convertibles. Mrs. Johnson and Texas Senator Ralph Yarborough sat in the back seat of another limousine, while the vice president rode in front with the driver.

President Kennedy's car led the motorcade, heading for Dallas to drum up support for the next election. A car of Secret Service agents followed, and Johnson's car was third.

Crowds lining the streets clapped and waved to the people in the cars and threw confetti. Johnson was relieved because he knew lots of people in Dallas hated him and Kennedy. Among other things, these people were angry about new laws Johnson had helped pass that gave African Americans more rights.

At 12:29 P.M. the parade of cars turned at the corner of Elm and Houston, and the road sloped down. Suddenly, a loud popping noise was heard.

"Get down!" yelled a Secret Service agent, who leaped over the seat to push Johnson to the floor and land on top of him. The vice president groaned as his shoulder hit the floorboard.

"Halfback! Halfback to Lawson!" the car radio crackled. "The president's been hit! Get us to a hospital, fast but safe."

With a powerful surge, the limo accelerated and raced off. Faster and faster they went, screeching around corners, until they lurched to a stop at Dallas Parkland Hospital. The car Kennedy had been riding in was just ahead of them.

Only then did Johnson learn that the president had been shot in the head. The Texas governor had also taken a bullet, but he was not as badly injured.

Secret Service agents, friends, and members of Congress milled around a trauma room lined with white sheets, where Johnson waited to learn Kennedy's fate.

The vice president remained quiet as questions ricocheted around the room about who had shot Kennedy. Was the shooting part of a plot? Would Johnson also be attacked?

"Where's the black bag?" the president's advisors wanted to know. This bag carried the codes to be used in case of a nuclear attack. Eventually the bag was found, but Johnson was too stunned to notice.

At 1:22 P.M. Kennedy's appointment secretary came in and said, "He's gone." At that point Lyndon Johnson was asked to take over the duties of a fallen president, just as the Constitution of the United States dictated.

Johnson had wanted to be president for a long time but not this way. He'd hoped to be nominated for the top spot in the 1960 election, but on the first convention ballot, Kennedy had 806 votes to Johnson's 409.

When Kennedy asked Johnson to run for the vice presidency, Johnson's friends were sure he would say no. After all, Johnson was the majority leader of the Senate. He decided which senators sat on which committees, and he could get laws passed that others thought were doomed. His brand of "flattery, threats, [and] reminders of past favors" was notorious as the "Johnson Treatment." Why should he settle for being just another vice president named Johnson in a job with no power at all?

Why, indeed? Perhaps because Sam Rayburn, the powerful Speaker of the House, convinced Johnson that if he didn't run with Kennedy, Richard Nixon would win the presidency. Perhaps Johnson's wife begged him to take things easier since he'd already suffered a heart attack.

And why did Kennedy pick Johnson? That answer is clearer. Kennedy was following the old tradition of **balancing the ticket.** If one candidate is from the North, tradition dictated that the other candidate be from the South. Kennedy, from Massachusetts, thought a Texan was just what he needed. This form of balancing the **ticket** dated back to when George Washington from Virginia served with John Adams from Massachusetts.

And Johnson also tended to balance the ticket in another time-honored way. As a power in the senate, Johnson was known as an **insider,** or one who could get laws passed. Kennedy, a relative newcomer to the Senate, was still looked at by some as an **outsider.**

A third method of balancing the ticket often relied on pairing a conservative and a liberal to get votes from the entire political party. Both Kennedy and Johnson, however, were seen as liberals.

None of these methods addressed whether the two men chosen liked each other or could work together. In fact, some presidents and vice presidents couldn't stand each other and refused to work together.

As **running mates,** Kennedy and Johnson didn't hate each other, but before they were even elected, differences were apparent. The Kennedys were extremely rich and sophisticated, while the Johnsons were used to a homey Texas lifestyle. In private, each side made fun of the other side's accent. Rumor had it that Mrs. Kennedy referred to the Johnsons as "Senator Cornpone and Mrs. Pork Chop."

The Johnsons were unpopular even in parts of Texas, particularly in Dallas. Four days before the 1960 election they were met by angry Nixon supporters in that city. Since the majority of the demonstrators were married to rich businessmen, most wore fur coats. They were quickly dubbed "the Mink Coat Mob," and they were aggressive.

When Johnson and his wife tried to cross the street to their hotel, one heckler spit at Mrs. Johnson and hit her over the head with a sign that said, "Let's Ground Lady Bird."

Mrs. Johnson started to yell back at the woman, but her husband quickly covered Lady Bird's mouth, shielded her, and steered her toward the hotel. More demonstrators waited inside, but with TV cameras rolling, the Johnsons forged ahead. Later Johnson made political points on the incident by playing to the southern code of chivalry toward women.

He said, "If the time has come that I can't walk with my lady through the corridors of the hotels of Dallas, then I want to know about it." Partly because of this episode, Kennedy and Johnson carried Texas, a key state in winning the election.

Johnson, seen here with his wife Lady Bird, used an attack against his wife to help support his ticket with Kennedy. The incident involving his wife in Dallas was considered one of the key moments in helping Kennedy and Johnson take the state of Texas.

Johnson knew that vice presidents had historically been powerless, but he said, "Power is where power goes." He assumed he could still **preside** at the Democratic **caucus** in the Senate, but he was wrong. The senators firmly reminded him that the Constitution called for separation between the executive branch and the Senate. Albert Gore Sr., father of our 45th vice president, declared, "This caucus is not open to former senators." Johnson was very upset at this rejection.

Soon Kennedy sent him to France, Senegal, China, India, Pakistan, Vietnam, and the Philippines on goodwill tours. Johnson was normally expected to do little except shake hands and be nice. But one exception came in 1961 when Communists challenged the right to travel through East Germany to get to the free side of West Berlin.

President Kennedy sent troops to try to drive through the blockades, and he sent Johnson to West Berlin to wait for the troops. This was a sign to the Communists that America meant business. When the troops arrived, Johnson looked like a hero.

At home Kennedy appointed Johnson chairman of the National Space Council. Johnson insisted the organization be properly funded, which made it possible for America to land a man on the moon sooner than it could have otherwise. The vice president was also made chairman of the Committee on Equal Employment, where he focused on trying to eliminate racial discrimination in the workplace.

These duties, plus meeting with the president's cabinet and attending meetings of the National Security Council, might have kept most men busy enough but not Johnson. He missed the rough and tumble process of getting laws passed. As a result he was often depressed and spent whole days in bed staring at the ceiling.

Shortly before the trip to Dallas in November 1963, Johnson faced new problems when some old business deals came back to haunt him. His friend Bobby Baker was charged with using his position in the Senate to make money, and Baker had to appear before a Senate committee. In 1957 Baker had sold Johnson a $100,000 life insurance policy, but Johnson, who had had a heart attack, should not have been able to get this insurance. Later Johnson was allowed to buy another $100,000 policy, and each time Baker collected a hefty fee for his salesmanship.

At almost the same time Kennedy was being shot in Dallas, the Senate was hearing testimony that could have been very embarrassing to Johnson. Once Johnson became

president, however, the issue of his connections to Baker were all but forgotten.

At about 2:25 P.M., after the shooting, Vice President Johnson, Lady Bird Johnson, Mrs. Kennedy, and Kennedy's body were back on *Air Force One.* Here Judge Sarah T. Hughes heard Johnson repeat the oath of office, making him the 36th president of the United States. Minutes later, the big plane took off for Washington, carrying Johnson to his destiny.

The men who wrote our Constitution were wise to make sure that a vice president would be ready to take over when there was a tragedy. This plan guaranteed an orderly transfer of power rather than chaos at such a time. But what does the vice president's job ask of him besides acting as a "president in waiting?" People have been asking this question for over 200 years.

Lyndon B. Johnson is sworn in as president aboard Air Force One, *following the assassination of President John F. Kennedy. The vice president serves many purposes and is the first in line to assume the presidency should circumstances call for it.*

We the People

of the United States, in order to form a more perfect Union, establish Justice, insure domestic Tranquility, provide for the common defence, promote the general Welfare, and secure the Blessings of Liberty to ourselves and our Posterity, do ordain and establish this Constitution for the United States of America.

Article I.

Article II.

Article III.

Article IV.

Article V.

Article VI.

Article VII.

done in Convention by the Unanimous Consent of the States present the Seventeenth Day of September in the Year of our Lord one thousand seven hundred and Eighty seven and of the Independance of the United States of America the Twelfth. **In Witness** whereof We have hereunto subscribed our Names,

Attest William Jackson Secretary

G⁰. Washington—Presid' and deputy from Virginia

Delaware
- Geo: Read
- Gunning Bedford jun
- John Dickinson
- Richard Bassett
- Jaco: Broom

Maryland
- James M:Henry
- Dan of S' Tho' Jenifer
- Dan' Carroll

Virginia
- John Blair—
- James Madison Jr.

North Carolina
- W" Blount
- Rich'd Dobbs Spaight
- Hu Williamson

South Carolina
- J. Rutledge
- Charles Cotesworth Pinckney
- Charles Pinckney
- Pierce Butler

Georgia
- William Few
- Abr Baldwin

New Hampshire
- John Langdon
- Nicholas Gilman

Massachusetts
- Nathaniel Gorham
- Rufus King

Connecticut
- W" Sam' Johnson
- Roger Sherman

New York
- Alexander Hamilton

New Jersey
- Wil: Livingston
- David Brearley
- W" Paterson
- Jona: Dayton

Pennsylvania
- B Franklin
- Thomas Mifflin
- Rob' Morris
- Geo. Clymer
- Tho' FitzSimons
- Jared Ingersoll
- James Wilson
- Gouv Morris

EXPLANATORY NOTES: This is an authentic copy of the contents of the Constitution of the United States, but the printing size of the text of the Articles has been reduced, and printed in two columns, in order to confine it to this sheet. It would take four sheets this size to make the entire text legible.

Following is a brief synopsis of the Articles: **ARTICLE I.—LEGISLATIVE DEPARTMENT:** How Senators and Representatives shall be chosen, and when they are to meet; Rules of procedure, compensation, privileges and immunities; Mode of passing laws, Powers granted to Congress; Powers denied to the Federal Government; Powers denied to the States. **ARTICLE II.—EXECUTIVE DEPARTMENT:** President and Vice-President; Powers and duties of the President; Impeachment. **ARTICLE III.—JUDICIAL DEPARTMENT:** The Federal Courts; Jurisdiction of the Federal Courts; Treason. **ARTICLE IV.—THE STATES AND THE FEDERAL GOVERNMENT:** State Records; Privileges and Immunities of Citizens; New States and Territories; Guarantees to the States. **ARTICLE V.—METHOD OF AMENDMENT.** Article VI.—PUBLIC DEBT; SUPREMACY OF THE CONSTITUTION; OATH OF OFFICE; no religious test required. ARTICLE VII.—RATIFICATION OF THE CONSTITUTION.

The original duties of the vice presidency are described in the U.S. Constitution. Although the responsibilities of the vice president have grown over the years, the groundwork laid by the Constitution remains the basis from which the vice president works.

CHAPTER 2

Founding Fathers: 1789–1805

IN 1787 THE REVOLUTIONARY WAR was over, and each of the 13 states had agreed to a "firm league of friendship" with its neighbors, but together they were not really a nation. No one could make them pay taxes, and some states were printing worthless money. Things were wildly disorganized.

George Washington and other leaders called a meeting to bring more order. Rhode Island refused to come, but by the end of May, enough delegates from the other 12 states had arrived at Philadelphia to begin.

Countless ideas were suggested for improving the old Articles of Confederation, but none pleased everyone. At last the delegates gave up and decided to create a whole new government.

Soon those who believed the federal government should have more power than individual states (the Federalists) were arguing with those who felt the opposite (the Anti-Federalists). As a compromise, they created a Senate, in which each state would get two votes, and a House of Representatives, in which larger states would get more votes. These two arms of Congress would pass the laws. A Supreme Court would make sure those laws followed the Constitution.

Delegates agreed that a separate executive arm would have a president to run the nation, but that left them with at least three more problems:

1. How should the president be elected?
2. How should the head of the Senate be chosen?
3. And how should a president who couldn't serve be replaced?

The states already had their own governments in place, and five had lieutenant governors who acted as governor when needed. In New York, the lieutenant governor presided in the state senate and cast a vote in case of ties.

The delegates used these models to create the federal vice presidency. They gave this office only two duties:

1. To preside in the Senate and vote in case of ties, and
2. To take over the president's duties if that person is unable to function.

Elbridge Gerry of Massachusetts was against this plan, though. He said that a vice president would be part of the executive branch and so should not get involved in what Congress did.

This was a good argument, but Roger Sherman of Connecticut pointed out: "If the vice-President were not to be President of the Senate, he would be without employment." The other delegates agreed and went ahead with their plan.

They decided the vice president should meet the same qualifications as the president: he must be born in

America, be at least 35 years old, and have lived in the United States for at least 14 years.

Each state would vote for president and use this popular vote to decide for whom to cast its electoral votes in the **electoral college.** The man with the most votes would be president; the runner-up would be vice president.

John Adams, an important leader in the American Revolution, was in England while the Constitution was being drawn up. When he came home in 1788, many people said that he should be vice president. Adams had several rivals for the job, however.

John Hancock only supported the new Constitution because he had been promised the job. Alexander Hamilton, leader of the Federalists while Adams was gone, wanted it too. Hamilton even had a friend suggest that Adams was too big a man in his own right to serve under Washington.

When Adams refused to fall for this flattery, Hamilton tried another scheme to cut Adams down to size. He asked certain states to vote for someone besides Adams with their second vote. Hamilton said that if Washington and Adams got an equal number of votes, Washington might not be the clear-cut choice for president.

The vote was 69 for Washington and only 34 for Adams. Upon seeing how poorly he had done, Adams wanted to forget about being vice president, but he felt it was his duty to serve. So he set off for New York, the U.S. capital at that time, with the promise of a $5,000-a-year salary. He would have to find his own place to live and pay all his other expenses out of that salary.

Adams got to New York before Washington and took charge of the Senate. Realizing that every move he made might set a **precedent,** he began by taking a vote on who should bow to whom when messengers came from the House of Representatives.

Then he insisted the Senate discuss the president's title. Adams, the Federalist, suggested they call him "His

John Adams was the country's first vice president. As many vice presidents have since done, Adams later became president himself.

Highness, the President of the United States of America and Protector of the Rights of the Same."

Most senators thought this idea and all Adam's worries about titles were ridiculous. James Madison led a successful campaign to simply call the new head of government "the president of the United States."

When Washington arrived, Adams had new worries. "Gentlemen," he said, "the President will, I suppose, address the **Congress.** How shall I behave? . . . Shall I be standing or sitting?" Hardly anyone cared, but some tried to remember what the British did in such situations.

When the big day arrived, Adams showed Washington to a chair and said that Washington should now take the presidential oath. Then Adams just stood there for a long time trying to remember his speech.

Finally he bowed and took Washington to the chief justice of New York, and the first president was sworn in.

Adams had to wait several more days for his own oath to be written so he could recite it.

No one told Adams that the vice presidency was supposed to be an unimportant office, so he took on duties that men who followed him never dreamed of. As head of the Senate, he made committee appointments, debated the bills that were introduced, and decided a record-breaking 29 tie votes. He was one of Washington's top advisors, sat in on all **cabinet** meetings and ran them when Washington was out of town. No other vice president did this until 1930.

Washington and Adams were reelected in 1792, so one might guess everyone was happy with things as they were. One would be wrong. Washington picked the best men available to run things, no matter what their beliefs, and this made for huge squabbles. Adams and Hamilton, the secretary of the treasury, were both Federalists, but Adams was jealous of Hamilton because Washington preferred Hamilton's advice to Adams's. Hamilton wanted to run the Federalist party and saw Adams as a rival.

Adams and Secretary of State Thomas Jefferson were longtime friends, despite Jefferson being an Anti-Federalist. But when Jefferson's book *Rights of Man* was published, it included a note that was not supposed to be printed. The playful note referred to earlier "heresies," and everyone knew Jefferson meant Adams's writings. Adams thought he'd been stabbed in the back.

When the election of 1796 came along, Adams was the clear choice for president. He and Thomas Pickney from South Carolina ran against Thomas Jefferson and Aaron Burr.

Hamilton wanted Pickney to be president instead of Adams, so he encouraged northern electors to vote for Adams and Pickney equally. Hamilton figured that southern voters would favor Pickney, giving him more votes than Adams.

But the northern electors cast 18 votes that were not for either Adams or Pickney, and Adams won with

71 votes. Jefferson, with 68 votes, was the new vice president.

Adams immediately asked Jefferson, who had worked with the French, to go to Paris for him. But Jefferson said, "The vice president . . . is too high a personage to be sent on diplomatic errands."

When Adams asked Jefferson to sit in on cabinet meetings, Jefferson said, "I consider my office as constitutionally confined to legislative functions." In other words, he was part of Congress rather than the president's man.

The hard feelings between Adams and Jefferson were such a problem that, in 1797, a new **amendment** to the Constitution was suggested. This amendment proposed to set up separate elections for president and vice president. Supporters hoped this amendment would make sure that two men with such different outlooks would not serve together in the future. The bill did not pass.

Although Jefferson worked against Adams most of the time, he did keep order in the Senate, not an easy job before the rules were established. In fact, one of Jefferson's most important contributions as vice president was in writing his *Manual of Parliamentary Practice*.

Adams and Jefferson continued to bicker, but in 1798, they went at each other even harder. Adams got a bill called the Alien and Sedition Acts passed. This bill made it a crime to speak out against the government. This law was obviously unconstitutional, since it denied free speech, but Adams couldn't see that.

When the government began to jail authors and editors and public speakers, Jefferson fought back. He wrote his "Kentucky Resolves," which asked the states not to enforce the new law. (The law was repealed in 1801.)

Adams ran for reelection in 1800, but because the votes for president and vice president were still done together, things got even messier. Both sides were so worried about a tie between their presidential and vice presidential candidates that certain electors were asked not to vote. In the

Soon after being dropped as vice president from Jefferson's ticket, Aaron Burr challenged Alexander Hamilton to this duel with pistols. Burr is seen here mortally wounding Hamilton.

confusion, Adams got 65 votes, his running mate got 64, and the two Anti-Federalists, Jefferson and Aaron Burr, each got 73. This was a tie between two men of the same party.

It took the House of Representatives seven straight days and 36 ballots to give one man a majority. Angry Adams backers made a deal with Burr and voted for him. But Hamilton had long hated Burr and spread the word that his enemy was a "dangerous" and "despicable" character.

Jefferson eventually became president, with Burr as vice president. Their inauguration was the first to be held in the new capital city, Washington, D.C.

After the election fiasco, Congress passed the 12th Amendment, separating the votes for vice president and president. It was finally ratified by all the states in 1804.

Since Burr had proved so untrustworthy in the election, Jefferson refused to work with him. Burr did a good job as chairman of the Senate, but Jefferson still dropped him from the 1804 ticket. Later that year, Burr's ongoing feud with Alexander Hamilton got so bitter that Burr challenged Hamilton to a duel with pistols. Hamilton was shot and killed; Burr fled west.

These founding fathers made sure the office of the vice presidency was firmly established, but it would be up to others to shape its future.

Vice President John Tyler decided he was president after William Harrison died of pneumonia. This bold decision led to many attacks against his presidency.

CHAPTER 3

The "Do-Nothings": 1805–1897

AFTER THE 12TH AMENDMENT passed, presidential hopefuls looked down on the vice presidency. The quality of nominees dropped too, and the two men elected often still had problems getting along.

When Jefferson ran for reelection, he was paired with George Clinton, the popular governor of New York. Clinton, already 65 years old, still hoped the vice presidency would lead to the presidential nomination in 1808. Yet he complained about his job in the Senate: "Sitting three hours in the chair at a time was extremely fatiguing."

As it turned out, Clinton's party picked James Madison as its top candidate in the next election. This left Clinton with the vice presidency again, and he was angry—so angry, he refused to go to Madison's inauguration.

For much of his term, the 70-year-old Clinton probably had what we would call Alzheimer's disease. Other senators said he had "no intellect or memory."

In 1811, Clinton broke a tie, voting not to renew the Bank of the United States. This cut off money needed to fight the War of 1812, and he did this only because it was something Madison wanted. Vice President Clinton died before the end of his term and was not replaced until the next election. This set a precedent that was followed until 1967.

Madison's next vice president, Elbridge Gerry, at 68, was also an old man. He is remembered mainly for a word coined from his last name.

In 1811, Gerry redrew all the election districts in Massachusetts to give his party a majority in as many as possible. Gerry's critics said his squiggly lines looked like a salamander, and called his actions "gerrymandering." He, too, died before his term was up.

Daniel Tompkins, vice president under James Monroe, suffered because of Clinton's vote against the Bank of the United States. As governor of New York during the War of 1812, Tompkins had no federal money to pay his troops, so he paid them out of his own pocket. Unfortunately, he did not keep good records of what he'd done.

Later, when Tompkins asked New York to pay him back, his enemies said that Tompkins had cheated the state. Tompkins spent most of his term as vice president trying to get his money back rather than serving in the Senate. But John Taylor said, "There is nothing for him to do here, and any other man may preside in the Senate as well as he."

As Tompkins's troubles dragged on, he drank more and more. One senator wrote, "He was several times so drunk in the chair that he could with difficulty put the questions [to a vote]."

Finally in 1824, during his second term as vice president, Tompkins was found innocent, and New York paid him more than $90,000.

In 1824 John Calhoun was young, handsome, a gifted public speaker, and really wanted to be president. But when he saw that either Andrew Jackson or John Quincy

Adams (John Adams's son) was going to get the nomination, Calhoun convinced both men to pick him as vice president if they won.

Neither man got a majority, though, and the House of Representatives had to pick a winner. Although Jackson had more votes than Adams going in, Adams won. Immediately Calhoun accused President Adams of making a crooked deal with Speaker of the House Henry Clay in order to win.

In 1828 Calhoun was reelected, this time with President Andrew Jackson, and they got along well until Calhoun's wife started trouble. Mrs. Calhoun snubbed Peggy O'Neale, wife of the secretary of war, because of Mrs. O'Neale's social background. This made Jackson and his wife furious, and soon the whole town was taking sides.

Later, Jackson and Calhoun squared off over tariffs. Calhoun believed that the new taxes put on goods that went in and out of the country would ruin business for his southern friends. He argued against the tariffs without success and finally urged southern states not to pay the taxes. President Jackson promised military action to collect the tariffs if necessary.

Obviously Jackson wasn't going to support Calhoun's nomination for president, so before his term was over, Calhoun ran for the Senate. He then became the first vice president ever to resign from office.

Martin Van Buren was nominated for vice president because of Calhoun. Jackson had originally appointed Van Buren as minister to Britain, but when the Senate voted on the appointment, there was a tie. Calhoun, as vice president, voted against Van Buren.

In the next election Jackson decided to run with Van Buren. "The little magician," as Van Buren was called for his many tricky deals, was a big help in getting the needed votes.

While Van Buren was vice president, Congress fought viciously over the Bank of the United States. In fact, Van

Buren sat in the Senate with two loaded pistols at the ready. Surprisingly, he was still one of the first to claim the two-party system could be a good thing.

In 1836, Jackson got Van Buren nominated for the top spot on the ticket. Richard Johnson was picked to run with him because he supposedly had killed the American Indian leader Tecumseh, making him a hero.

But stories about Johnson's family soon raised eyebrows. People were shocked to learn that Johnson had fathered two daughters with a former slave. Although Van Buren won easily, Johnson did not get a majority, and the Senate was called in to choose a vice president. When Johnson finally got the job, he did practically nothing with it.

In 1840, John Tyler ran for vice president alongside 68-year-old war hero William Harrison. After Harrison's two-hour inauguration speech in a cold rain, he caught pneumonia and died a month later. Suddenly Tyler was president.

Or was he? The Constitution said that if the president could not serve, the vice president should "discharge the powers and duties of the said office." It did not say, "the vice president shall become president."

Tyler decided he *would* be the president. He took a new oath of office, moved into the White House, and gave an inaugural address. Immediately he was attacked from all sides for taking this bold step. Many refused to call him "Mr. President," preferring the title "His Accidency" instead.

Three days after Tyler took over, most of his cabinet quit, and soon his own party was calling for him to resign. Congress refused to even give Tyler the money to keep the White House in good condition. But Tyler stubbornly held on to set an important precedent.

George Dallas, who served under the next president, James Polk, is remembered mainly for breaking a tie vote in favor of the Tariff Act of 1846. Although his home state of Pennsylvania was aggressively against this law, Dallas felt it was for the good of the country as a whole. A city was also named after him when he helped bring Texas into the country.

When Vice President Millard Fillmore took over the Senate in 1849, he sometimes had to struggle to keep northern and southern senators from coming to blows. In 1850 Senator Henry Clay drew up a compromise to try to keep the peace. Fillmore was all for it; President Zachary Taylor was against it.

But in July of that year, President Taylor died of stomach ailments. Thanks to Tyler's earlier struggles, Fillmore was immediately accepted as president and was able to sign Clay's Compromise of 1850. This bill helped postpone the Civil War for another decade.

William King, the 13th vice president, was so sick when elected with President Franklin Pierce that Congress had to pass a special law to let him recite his oath of office in Cuba. King died without ever getting to Washington.

The next vice president, John Breckenridge, spent his whole term under President James Buchanan trying to stop the coming Civil War, but it broke out shortly after they left office in 1861. Breckenridge then became a brigadier general in the Confederate army.

Hannibal Hamlin of Maine, an outspoken foe of slavery, was chosen to balance the 1860 ticket with Abraham Lincoln of Illinois. He and Lincoln got along quite well until Lincoln sent Hamlin to ask William Seward to be secretary of state. Lincoln was sure his old enemy Seward would decline, but Hamlin goofed by convincing Seward to take the job.

Lincoln was so disgusted that he mostly ignored Hamlin for the rest of the term. Still, the president followed Hamlin's advice by letting African Americans join the Union army.

Andrew Johnson, the second vice president with that last name, was nominated for the office for Lincoln's second term as a reward for being the only Southern senator

Although John Breckenridge spent much of his time as vice president trying to avoid the Civil War, he later fought for the South as a brigadier general for the Confederacy.

to stay when his state left the Union. (Johnson was a Democrat, Lincoln a Republican.)

On inauguration day in 1865, Johnson was recovering from typhoid fever and feeling sick, so he took some whiskey, hoping it would help. Instead, the whiskey made him barely able to think or talk. History recorded him as being drunk at his own inauguration, even though President Lincoln said, "Andy ain't no drunkard."

The South surrendered that same year and the Civil War was over. Lincoln and Johnson believed that both sides had suffered enough. They were prepared to deal gently with the beaten rebels. But on April 14, 1865, a Southern extremist shot and killed President Lincoln. Another man was supposed to shoot Johnson at the same time, but that assassin apparently lost his nerve.

Now Johnson was left to reason with highly unreasonable people intent on severely punishing the South. He was in a constant battle with Congress, and the last straw seemed to be when he fired Secretary of War Edwin Stanton. The Senate illegally ordered Johnson to rehire Stanton, and Johnson refused. If he had allowed Congress to triumph, future presidents would have always been worried about being overruled by the legislative branch.

The first African-American military regiments were created in the Union army following the advice of Vice President Hannibal Hamlin while he served under President Abraham Lincoln.

But this strong stand caused the House of Representatives to **impeach** Johnson, and he missed being thrown out of office by only one vote.

Schuyler Colfax had a very forgettable term (1869–1873) as vice president under Ulysses S. Grant.

The next vice president, Henry Wilson, spent most of his time during Grant's second term writing a three-volume book called *History of the Rise and Fall of Slave Power in America.*

William Wheeler, who held office under President Rutherford Hayes from 1877–1881, likewise did little.

In 1865, John Wilkes Booth shot and killed President Lincoln. Serving as vice president, Andrew Johnson was soon sworn in as president but faced much adversity while serving as our country's highest official.

The next vice president, Chester Arthur, was known to be part of a corrupt New York political machine. His main reasons for being on the ticket were to win votes from die-hard supporters of Grant and to balance President James Garfield, who was from Ohio.

While others had looked down on the vice presidency, Arthur said it was "a greater honor than I have ever dreamed of attaining." Still, his main goal in that office was to get soft, high-paying jobs for his friends.

On July 2, 1881, four months after Arthur took office, President Garfield was shot and wounded so badly that he couldn't function as president. Arthur, having no constitutional authority to act, was afraid to do anything. So he stayed in New York and talked to the secretary of state regularly about Garfield's condition.

When Garfield died, the precedent Tyler had set allowed Arthur to become president without a hitch. Arthur asked Congress to pass a law to determine what should be done when a president is unable to act, but they failed to come up with one. Arthur did not choose a vice president to finish out the term.

Thomas Hendricks was in office with President Grover Cleveland for only nine months in 1885 before he died. Hendricks did nothing noteworthy in that time.

Levi Morton had turned down the vice presidential nomination in 1880, but he ran with Benjamin Harrison in 1888. Morton (in office from 1889–93) was known for his fairness to both his own Republicans and the outnumbered Democrats in the Senate.

Adlai Stevenson, our 23rd vice president, was not even told when his president, Grover Cleveland, had surgery for cancer. This top-secret procedure, performed aboard a yacht, removed part of Cleveland's upper jaw. But all Stevenson (not to be confused with his grandson, also named Adlai and also a politician) knew was that Cleveland was cruising on Long Island Sound.

The office of the vice presidency had gained very little power or prestige in its first hundred years. But there were changes ahead.

Theodore "Teddy" Roosevelt discovered the vice presidency wasn't nearly as exciting as the days he'd spent as a cowboy, outdoorsman, and soldier. His boredom would not last long as he was thrust into our country's most powerful position when President McKinley was assassinated.

CHAPTER 4

Some Livelier Leaders: 1897–1945

ACCORDING TO SENATOR HENRY Cabot Lodge, Garret Hobart "restored the Vice-Presidency to its proper position, and lifted it . . . to the dignity and importance which it merits."

Hobart, elected in 1896, was definitely a bigger help to his president (McKinley) than the three men who came before him. He invited congressmen to his house for card games and drinks and then convinced them to vote his way. Unfortunately, he died before his term was over.

Then came Theodore (Teddy) Roosevelt. Nominated when McKinley ran for reelection, Roosevelt was the most colorful vice presidential candidate ever. He had climbed mountains, worked as a cowboy, written books, and been a hero in the Spanish-American War.

He was also a dedicated public servant. As a young assemblyman, he had accused the enormously wealthy Jay Gould of trying to corrupt

President William McKinley was shot in 1901, and although it appeared he would recover from his wounds, he later died. Teddy Roosevelt was recalled from a hunting trip and sworn in as president in Buffalo, New York.

a Supreme Court justice. As president of New York City's police commissioners, he had walked the street to make sure that the police enforced the laws. As governor of New York, he had pressed big businessmen to pay their fair share of taxes.

But this kind of crusading made some Republicans very uneasy. So they decided to give Teddy the vice presidency to get him out of the way. Senator Mark Hanna saw the danger in this plan. He said, "Don't any of you realize there is only one life between this madman and the White House?"

Roosevelt enthusiastically traveled 21,209 miles during the 1900 reelection campaign. President McKinley, as was the custom, stayed home. But when Roosevelt's team won, he was so bored with his new post that he made plans to study law in his spare time.

Then, on September 6, 1901, the president was shot and wounded. The vice president rushed to McKinley's side only to be told the president was going to be fine.

Roosevelt went on a hunting trip in the Adirondack Mountains. He was 10 miles from the nearest road when a guide appeared with the news that McKinley was dying. Roosevelt hiked out, raced over dark, muddy mountain roads in a buggy, and caught a special train to Buffalo, New York. There, in the home of a local judge, he was sworn in as the new president.

In the 1904 election, the conservative Charles Fairbanks ran for vice president to balance the "radical" President Roosevelt. They were so poorly matched that, after they won, Fairbanks usually sided with Roosevelt's enemies.

Charles Sherman, the 27th vice president, was equally unhelpful. When President William Taft asked him to help get a bill through Congress, Sherman said, "Acting as a messenger boy is not part of the duties of a Vice President." Sherman was renominated with Taft but died before election day. The vote went ahead anyway, and the nation elected a dead man.

Thomas Marshall served for two terms (1913–1921) as vice president to Woodrow Wilson. He supported the president in the Senate and chaired the cabinet when Wilson was in Paris. But women seeking a constitutional amendment to give them the right to vote found him unsympathetic.

Many historians also criticize Marshall for not doing more when President Wilson became seriously ill in 1919. However, Marshall was not told the president had suffered a major stroke. The secretary of state begged Wilson's doctors to tell the truth, but instead, the doctors told the cabinet that the president had had a nervous breakdown.

The country had been without a leader for over a week when a newspaper reporter briefed Marshall on the true situation. Marshall wrote, "It was the first great shock of my life."

Finally the country learned that the president would be bedridden for "an extended period," and Marshall was urged to take over. Since the Constitution was unclear on this point, Marshall wanted to talk to the president about it. But Mrs. Wilson wouldn't let him. What was Marshall to do? He stood back and let others make the decisions.

While much of the country's business waited, Marshall spent his time entertaining important people from foreign countries. He even went on a speaking tour to help pay for these parties, since his $12,000 salary was too small.

Calvin Coolidge was an unlikely politician because he did not like to talk. Before he became vice president to Warren Harding in 1921, his only claim to fame was a statement he had made as governor of Massachusetts. After striking policemen in Boston were fired, riots broke out. Then the policemen wanted their jobs back. But Coolidge said: "There is no right to strike against the public safety by anybody, anywhere, any time."

Coolidge didn't even go to the Republican National Convention. When he was asked to run for vice president, his wife said, "You aren't going to take it are you?" Coolidge replied, "I suppose I'll have to."

Neither Coolidge nor his running mate, Warren Harding, did much campaigning, but Coolidge did manage to get out of New England for the second time in his life.

The Republicans won in a landslide, and Harding asked Coolidge to sit in as an official member of his cabinet. "Silent Cal" obliged, but he seldom took part. He was equally uninvolved with the Senate, and once when he saw a tough decision coming up, Coolidge walked out.

The Coolidges were not popular in Washington society, but they didn't care. The vice president liked 8–9 hours of sleep a night on top of his regular two-hour afternoon nap. When the couple did go out, it seemed Coolidge only went because "You gotta eat somewhere."

The vice president was asleep in his father's home in Vermont on October 2, 1923, when a courier pounded on

Another vice president to have tragedy lead to the presidency, Calvin Coolidge became president after Warren Harding died of a stroke. Although he did not enjoy public speaking, Coolidge performed the first presidential speech broadcast on radio.

the door to announce that Harding had died of a massive stroke. The new president's first message to Congress was also the first presidential speech ever broadcast on radio.

Charles Dawes was tapped for the second office when Coolidge ran for reelection in 1924. He had been a general in World War I, and his later "Dawes Plan" for handling German war payments made him a Nobel Peace Prize winner.

Coolidge expected the newly-elected Dawes to sit in on cabinet meetings just as he had. But, before Coolidge could invite him, Dawes sent the president a letter stating he would not attend. Dawes believed it was too dangerous, because if the president and the vice president were to disagree, the president couldn't fire his vice president. This letter angered Coolidge.

Dawes quickly made enemies in the Senate, too. First he lectured the senators on a law he didn't fully understand, and then he ruined the dignity of the senators' swearing-in ceremony by rushing them through in large groups.

Five days later, the Senate got even. When they were supposed to vote on the confirmation of Coolidge's nominee for attorney general, the senators told Dawes that there would be six more speakers before the vote came up.

Dawes fell for the bait and went back to his room to take a nap. Then all the speakers quickly dropped out except for one, and the senators were called to vote. Dawes heard about the change and raced back in a taxi cab, but he was too late. Coolidge's attorney general was not confirmed.

Charles Curtis, the 31st vice president, is the only person of Native American ancestry ever to serve in that office. President Hoover never gave him any assignments or asked Curtis to join in cabinet meetings, though.

About this time a musical on Broadway called *Of Thee I Sing* included a completely unknown and uninformed "Vice President Alexander Throttlebottom." Many thought Throttlebottom's situation summed up Curtis's.

John Garner, the vice president who took office in 1933, started out well. He faithfully attended cabinet meetings and tried to get President Franklin Roosevelt's "New Deal" policies through Congress. He was also the first vice president to represent the United States outside of the country when he visited both Japan and the Philippines. But he lacked the vision of his better-educated boss, so they did not always get along.

On February 6, 1933, the 20th Amendment to the Constitution was passed. It changed the inauguration date from early March to January 20th. This left outgoing presidents

THE MUSIC BOX

WILLIAM GAXTON, LOIS MORAN AND VICTOR MOORE

OF THEE I SING

The program for the musical Of Thee I Sing *says little of the rumors that one of the characters, Vice President Alexander Throttlebottom, seemed to be based on the situation of the real vice president, Charles Curtis.*

less time to serve as **"lame ducks."** It also said that the vice president-elect should take over if the president-elect died before taking office.

After Roosevelt and Garner were reelected, they began to drift farther apart, until they were downright hostile to one another. Garner (also known as "Cactus Jack") started spending his time on the front porch of his ranch house in Texas. He told reporters that the vice presidency was "not worth a bucket of warm spit."

Garner was very upset when Roosevelt decided to run for a third term, something not even George Washington had done. And Roosevelt was just as tired of Garner. So, as the nation headed toward World War II in 1940, Roosevelt picked a running mate as different from Garner as possible.

Troops storm the beaches of Iwo Jima during World War II. Vice President Henry Wallace was in charge of a board of politicians who helped stockpile weapons and supplies for the war.

Roosevelt chose his popular secretary of agriculture, Henry Wallace of Iowa. This was not an effort to balance the ticket but one to capture the farm vote.

Wallace, who had been a Republican just a few years earlier, was viewed with mistrust by the other Democrats. In fact, he wasn't even a politician; he was a scientist who worked with hybrid seed corn. Roosevelt had to threaten not to run to get Wallace nominated.

Before Wallace was even sworn in, Roosevelt sent the new vice president to Mexico, where he gave a speech in Spanish. In 1943 Wallace went on a tour of Latin America, and in 1944, he spent two months in Asia. These were huge steps toward getting the United States more involved in world affairs and toward giving the office of the vice presidency some prestige.

At home, Wallace was in charge of the Economic Defense Board, which stockpiled supplies that were used when the United States entered World War II on December 7, 1941. In addition, he served as an official member of the cabinet and headed up the new committee on atomic energy.

Wallace was clearly pushing the boundaries of what it meant to be a vice president, but he was also making enemies. He battled with the secretary of commerce and the secretary of state over who was in charge of various projects. Also, some said he underestimated the dangers of Communism.

So, even though Roosevelt's influential wife Eleanor strongly supported Wallace for reelection, Franklin Roosevelt was enough of a politician to see that he would need a new partner in the next election, his fourth.

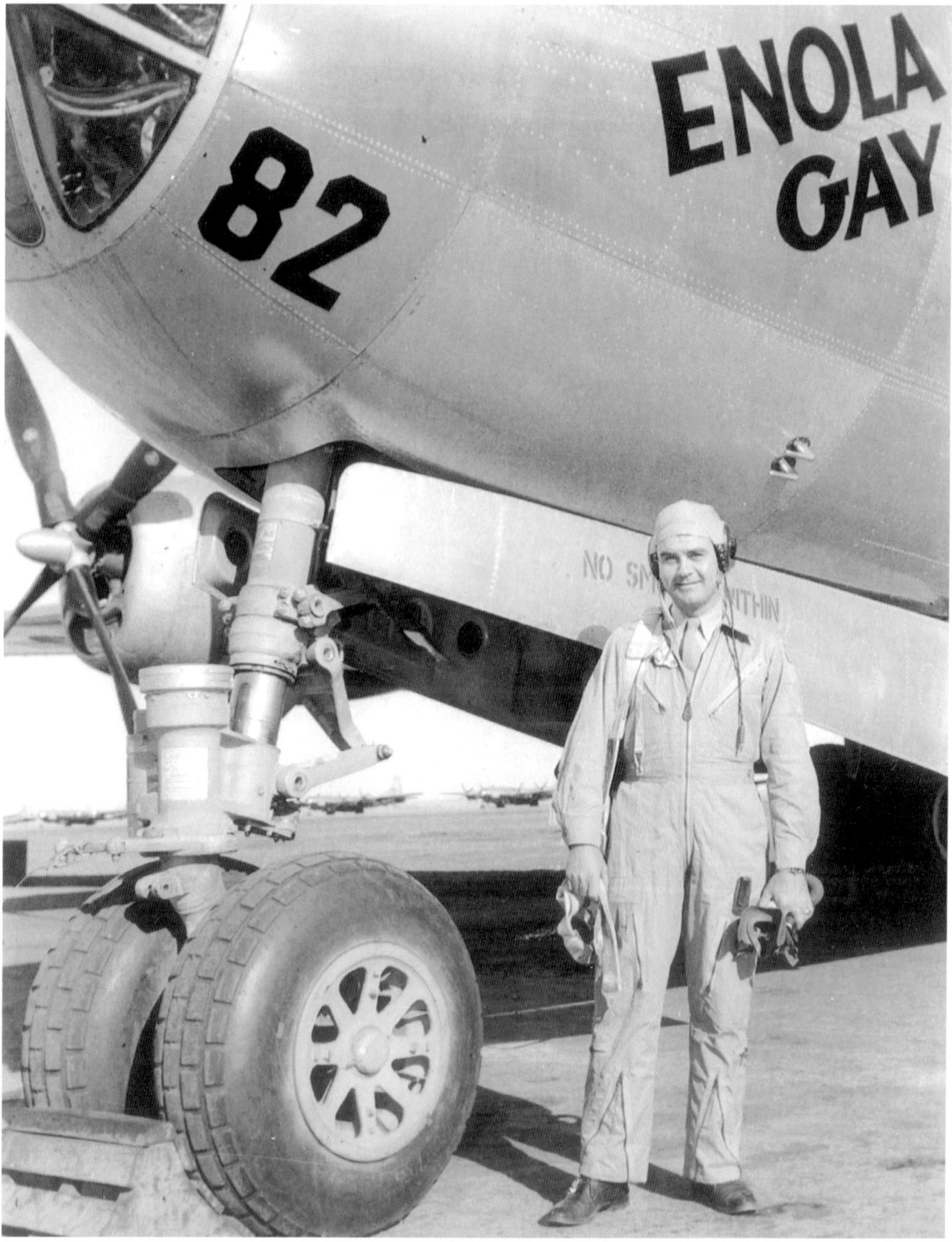
ENOLA GAY
82

Col. Paul W. Tibbets stands beside the B-29 Enola Gay, which dropped the atomic bomb on Hiroshima, Japan. Soon after President Franklin Roosevelt's death, successor Harry S. Truman ordered the first atomic bomb's use to help bring an end to World War II.

5

Men Severely Tested: 1945–68

HARRY S. TRUMAN OF MISSOURI did not want to be vice president and ran only because President Franklin Roosevelt insisted. Roosevelt's committee had considered several other names before Robert Hannigan, chairman of the Democratic Party, suggested Truman, a fellow "Show-Me-State" politician.

At first the committee members shook their heads. Sure, Truman was popular for his investigation of companies that provided war supplies and for saving taxpayers billions of dollars. But he was short, plain looking, wore steel-rimmed glasses, and had an unpleasant speaking voice. He just didn't look or sound like a president.

Only after the Democrats got to their convention in 1944 did Truman begin to emerge as a compromise **nominee.** Truman still kept resisting.

The night before the vote, Roosevelt called Hannigan and asked, "Have you got that fellow [Truman] lined up yet?" Hannigan said,

"No, he is the contrariest Missouri mule I've ever dealt with."

"Well," said Roosevelt, "you tell him, if he wants to break up the Democratic party in the middle of the war, that's his responsibility." So, with thoughts of American soldiers dying in Europe, Truman agreed to run.

As vice president, Truman only met in private with Roosevelt three times. His job was to promote Roosevelt's policies in the Senate and to make public appearances for the wheelchair-bound president. Truman learned nothing about running the country, nor was he given any special information on how World War II was progressing.

But on April 12, 1945, Eleanor Roosevelt called to say that the president was dead. Without warning, Harry Truman was leader of a country fighting a world war. He told people he felt as if a load of hay had fallen on him, and he asked for their prayers.

It was two weeks after he became president that Truman heard about an awesome new weapon with the power of 20,000 tons of TNT: the atomic bomb. Soon Truman had to weigh the facts and decide whether to use the bomb. Germany surrendered on May 7, but the Japanese continued to kill Americans at an alarming rate. Truman's advisors told him that a million more allied troops might die if they had to invade Japan.

On August 6, 1945, Truman gave the order that caused instant death to 80,000 people and a slower death to 90,000 more in Hiroshima, Japan. An even more powerful bomb was dropped on the city of Nagasaki on August 9, and the war was over.

Truman faced enormous challenges throughout his term as president, and it's a miracle he met them as well as he did with no prior training. His "trial by fire" made people begin to see the vice presidency in a different light.

Since the nation had no vice president for the next four years, Truman continued to make the difficult decisions alone. Some of these choices hurt Truman's popularity, and Democrats doubted he could retake the presidency in 1948. No one seemed interested in being his running mate.

Then Alben Barkley, the 71-year-old minority leader of the Senate, asked Truman for the nomination, and Truman agreed. Like candidates before him, Truman went chugging across the country on a train, but Barkley was the first to fly to his campaign speaking engagements.

The pair fooled everyone. They pulled a surprise upset over Republican candidate Thomas Dewey. Barkley became the oldest vice president ever.

President Truman wanted Barkley to be more prepared to take over as president than he had been. At Truman's urging, Congress passed a law making the vice president a member of the National Security Council. This council, created in 1947, kept track of threats from abroad. Barkley went to NSC meetings, but he didn't say much.

He was more helpful in the Senate, where he pushed President Truman's policies. Often, however, Barkley was writing love letters during the debates, and he married Jane Hadley on November 18, 1949.

This romance charmed the ladies of the country, and Barkley's sense of humor made him a very popular vice president. Truman rewarded Barkley by ordering that a vice presidential flag and seal be created.

The general who presented the flag to Barkley said, "I do not know whether the eagle on this flag is a male eagle or a female eagle." The vice president replied, "What difference would that make except to another eagle?"

Barkley's young grandson added a new word to the language when he called his grandfather the "Veep."

In 1951, the Republicans in Congress, remembering how Roosevelt had won four elections, pushed through the 22nd Amendment to the Constitution. This amendment limits a president to two terms, and it cuts down on rivalry between presidents and vice presidents who might both want to run for the top slot.

That same year, Dewey, still a powerful political leader, decided that General Dwight Eisenhower would be the Republican candidate for president. In looking for a vice president, his attention fell on Richard Nixon, then the youngest Republican in the Senate.

Dewey figured that Senator Nixon could run on his reputation as an anti-Communist crusader and serve as "insider" to "outsider" Eisenhower. In addition, the fiery young senator's style would offset that of the aging Eisenhower, who liked to pretend he was above politics. In other words, Dewey expected Nixon to serve as "hatchet man" in dealing with negative comments about the administration.

Before 1960, vice presidents had no paid speech writers, so it was understood that Nixon would need certain talents for the job. He proved himself before the campaign even got started. When it was reported that Nixon had taken money from favor-seeking millionaires, Republican leaders wanted to dump him.

Nixon fought back with a speech over nationwide TV in which he assured everyone that the only gift he had received was a cocker spaniel named Checkers. The "Checkers speech" made him an overnight celebrity.

At Nixon's inauguration in 1953, he was only 39, the youngest vice president ever elected. During his eight years serving under Eisenhower, he greatly strengthened the office of the vice president. Nixon was especially active in dealing with foreign leaders, and he didn't just shake hands: he talked business with them.

His first trip to Asia opened new doors to Communist China, and his later tours of Vietnam and South Korea inspired him to suggest new policies to the president. In Peru and Venezuela in 1958, he faced mobs so angry at the United States that they threw rocks at him. On a trip

Vice President Richard Nixon is shown with his dog, Checkers, in 1959. Nixon's "Checkers speech" saved his political career by helping him regain the support of the Republican Party and earned him overnight recognition with the public.

to Moscow in 1959, Nixon debated capitalism versus Communism with Soviet leader Nikita Khrushchev.

If President Eisenhower was out of town, Nixon led cabinet meetings and the National Security Council. When Eisenhower suffered a heart attack in 1955, Nixon took over most of Eisenhower's duties. Still, the Constitution's vagueness in this area made Nixon afraid to take on too much power.

Eisenhower begged Congress in 1956 and 1957 to help settle this issue, but they failed to come up with a new amendment.

In 1959 Nixon was the first vice president since Teddy Roosevelt to be automatically chosen as his party's presidential candidate. He was the heavy favorite against the Democrats' relatively unknown Senator John Kennedy.

But this time, TV was Nixon's downfall. When the two staged a debate during prime time, Kennedy won the hearts of Americans. After the election Kennedy continued to enjoy a high level of public confidence until his seemingly charmed life was ended by an assassin's bullet. Vice President Lyndon Johnson succeeded him.

As the next elections approached in 1964, President Johnson, the Texan, chose Hubert Humphrey from Minnesota to run with him. Senator Humphrey, a powerful liberal, favored arms control pacts with the Soviet Union, federal aid for education, and civil rights. Johnson knew Humphrey was qualified to be a president, and when they took office, Johnson promised that Humphrey would be the most active vice president in history.

Humphrey worked hard and helped push Johnson's "Great Society" programs through the Senate. He chaired many committees and served as an advisor to the president on foreign affairs. He worked right alongside the president— until he told Johnson something he didn't want to hear.

In 1965 our country was being increasingly drawn into war in Vietnam. A Vietcong attack on a U.S. compound in February of that year killed nine and wounded more than 100. Most of Johnson's advisors said the United States should bomb North Vietnam in response. Humphrey, however, put together a long, carefully thought-out paper arguing against getting more involved in the war.

Suddenly Humphrey was out in the cold. He was not invited to important meetings, and even though he was a member of the National Security Council by law, Johnson called secret meetings that did not include Humphrey.

Johnson found other ways to humiliate the vice president, too. He wouldn't let Humphrey represent the United States at the funeral of Winston Churchill. He called

Humphrey to his office and made him repeat speeches word-for-word that he'd already given. He even invited Humphrey to his ranch and put the vice president on a horse that he couldn't handle.

Though Humphrey was no longer getting the real story about Vietnam, he had to keep defending the unpopular war. Evidence indicated that Nixon, still an active Republican, had told the North Vietnamese not to ask for peace until after the next election. It was said that Nixon had promised to give the Vietcong better peace terms if he became president. These were serious charges, and Humphrey begged Johnson to make this plot public. Johnson wouldn't do it.

In 1967, Congress finally passed the 25th Amendment to the Constitution, putting rules in place about when and how a vice president should act if a president is unable to serve. The new amendment also gave the president the authority to appoint a new vice president, subject to approval by Congress.

The past 20 years had been tough on vice presidents, but a lot of progress was made.

As the war in Vietnam escalated, Vice President Hubert Humphrey argued against the United States' involvement in the conflict. Following his comments, Humphrey found himself at odds with President Lyndon Johnson and accomplished little.

Vice President Al Gore, at right, speaks with President Clinton at a campaign stop in 1999. In modern times, the vice presidency plays a far more important role in our government than the position once did.

CHAPTER 6

Modern Vice Presidents: 1968–2000

IN 1968, FORMER VICE President Nixon was nominated for president and chose Maryland's governor, Spiro Agnew, to run with him. Perhaps Nixon made this choice because some Republicans were calling for stronger action against antiwar demonstrators. These more radical conservatives were also suspicious of minorities.

Agnew quickly made news. He refused to campaign in the inner cities, saying, "When you've seen one slum, you've seen them all." He called a reporter of Japanese descent a derogatory name. He angered Polish Americans by referring to them as "Polacks." Sadly, his unkind remarks caused many to label him "Spiro our Hero" and to vote Republican.

Next he accused the media of not reporting the news fairly. And he said college professors were "poisoning the minds of the nation's young." Still he remained popular with certain groups.

The Watergate complex was the center of a controversy which forced President Richard Nixon from office. Unaware of the president's guilt, Vice President Gerald Ford defended the president until Nixon's involvement became obvious, and he left office.

Nixon ran with Agnew again in 1972, and they were reelected in a landslide. But then Agnew's past began to catch up with him. It was reported that as governor of Maryland, Agnew had taken bribes. Also, he had failed to report this money on his income tax.

In October of 1973 Agnew pleaded "no contest" to the charges and resigned as vice president. This was the second time in our nation's history that a vice president quit his post, but Angew was the first to do so because of criminal charges.

Soon the Republicans faced even bigger problems. The word "Watergate," and the charges that went with it, became the talk of the country.

Although Nixon claimed he was innocent, it appeared he had been part of a plot to put secret microphones inside Democratic headquarters in Washington, D.C., in 1972. Watergate was the name of the office complex where five intruders, who were obviously involved in illegal activities, had been caught.

Even while he fought for his political life, Nixon used the 25th Amendment to pick Agnew's replacement. On December 6, 1973, Congress overwhelmingly approved Senator Gerald Ford as vice president. He was the first to be appointed rather than elected.

Ford hoped Nixon was innocent and loyally gave speeches in which he said exactly what he was told to say. But nine months after Ford took office, it was obvious that Nixon had been involved in the Watergate scandal. He had broken even more laws in covering up his crimes for two years.

Nixon resigned on August 9, 1974, and Ford became the nation's 38th president. Then Ford used the 25th Amendment to choose Nelson Rockefeller, former governor of New York, for vice president.

Rockefeller, grandson of an oil millionaire, wanted to be president—*not* vice president. Rockefeller knew that if he became vice president, with Ford poised to run for the top spot in 1976, Rockefeller would probably never have another chance at the presidency.

Yet the country was in such a sorry state that Rockefeller told his friend James Cannon, "You know how I feel about being Vice President. . . . I will do this for President Ford, and through him, for the country."

After assuming office, Ford asked Rockefeller to be in charge of normal, everyday things that went on in the country, and Rockefeller agreed. But this plan was unworkable. Ford was committed to shrinking the government and saving money. Rockefeller, on the other hand, wanted to help people, and that takes money.

Although he was vice president for barely more than a year, Rockefeller did investigate the Central Intelligence Agency (CIA) and cause the Senate to reconsider its tradition of unlimited debate. He was not nominated for office in 1976.

Walter Mondale was the first vice presidential candidate to appear in a TV debate with his opponent. When he and President Jimmy Carter took office, they set new standards for teamwork.

Mondale said he wanted to be "general advisor to the president." Carter agreed. Mondale asked to be "in the loop" with an office in the west wing of the White House in addition to offices in the Executive Office Building as other vice presidents had had. Carter agreed.

As a Mondale advisor explained, "Most of the [country's] business is done by floating in and out of each other's offices. . . . If you are out of the loop, it is very hard to be part of the process." Later Dan Quayle, vice president under George Bush, said, "It signaled the most significant change in the power and influence of the vice presidency since the position was created."

Mondale helped Carter pick his cabinet and staff and shared his ideas with the president in private. He also served as a peacemaker between Jimmy Carter and the Senate and later between Egypt and Israel.

But Mondale was deeply committed to making people's lives easier, and just as Rockefeller had fought with Ford on this issue, Mondale eventually grew impatient with Carter. When oil shortages caused much higher gas prices in 1979, Mondale asked Carter to spend some money on the problem. Carter refused.

Eventually Mondale felt almost powerless as had earlier vice presidents. A staff member described him as being "despondent" and "heartbroken." Yet he continued to be his boss's chief cheerleader, whether he agreed with his ideas or not.

Carter and Mondale lost to Ronald Reagan and George Bush in 1980. But Mondale did something very unique, even in defeat. He showed Bush and his staff everything he'd learned about teamwork at the top, and Bush took this advice, particularly in keeping his main office in the White House.

Reagan immediately put Bush in charge of a new "Task Force on Regulatory Relief." Bush was delighted, because he agreed that U.S. industries needed relief from some of the new health and safety laws that were expensive to meet. As head of this task force, Bush let carmakers postpone installing air bags and having to invent new cars that burned unleaded gas.

At first Reagan's people worried that Bush wanted too much power for himself. But on March 30, 1981, President Reagan was shot and wounded. When Bush, who was in Texas, rushed back to Washington, D.C., his staff urged him to land on the south lawn of the White House. Bush vetoed the idea, saying, "Only the president lands on the south lawn."

The next day Bush carried on the business of the country, but he did not sit in Reagan's chair. His actions reassured everyone that the vice president was not trying to take over. In 1985, Bush was again acting president while Reagan had cancer surgery.

Foreign affairs were one of Bush's specialties, particularly attending funerals. People joked about how many he went to, but funerals were actually good places to meet with the leaders of other countries. He handled delicate negotiations with Communist China over guns and with El Salvador over human rights violations. He also got acquainted with each of three successive new leaders of the Soviet Union.

In 1984, the Democrats nominated Geraldine Ferraro as the first woman to run for vice president (with Walter Mondale), but Reagan and Bush were easily reelected.

Only one scandal threatened Bush's reputation. In 1986 it was learned that guns had been sold to Iran (which had held American hostages in 1979–81) to get money for

Vice President Dan Quayle will probably be remembered more for his blunders than for anything else. Although the vice president had the unfortunate habit of sticking his foot in his mouth, he did perform a number of valuable services for the country.

the anticommunists in Nicaragua. Bush, however, could claim he knew nothing about it since he had missed two key National Security Council meetings.

In 1988, Bush ran for president, and he picked 41-year-old Senator Dan Quayle from Indiana as a running mate. Soon many were wondering why.

Quayle had no experience in the national limelight, so he occasionally embarrassed himself. For example, during a TV debate he drew angry criticism by comparing himself to the much-loved President John F. Kennedy.

Bush won the election in spite of Quayle, and the young vice president worked hard to repay Bush's confidence. Quayle succeeded in shepherding several bills through the Senate for Bush and managed to get a re-designed space station approved despite the National Academy of Science's objections.

But in his numerous public appearances, Quayle still put his foot in his mouth. At a United Negro College Fund event he confused their slogan "A mind is a terrible thing to waste." Instead, Quayle said, "What a waste it is to lose one's mind."

In 1991, he angered the American Bar Association by suggesting that lawyers charge too much. In 1992, he attacked the TV show *Murphy Brown* because it portrayed motherhood for unmarried women. Quayle's point was that a two-parent family is better, but his message got lost in a storm of ridicule.

The 1992 election winners were Democrats Bill Clinton of Arkansas and Al Gore of Tennessee. This ticket was not balanced by geography. But Senator Gore, an insider, was expected to help Governor Clinton, an outsider, deal with Congress.

One of Gore's first assignments as vice president was to examine each department of government to make it work more efficiently. He came up with two forklifts' worth of wasteful government regulations and predicted that eliminating them would save taxpayers $108 billion over the next five years.

In 1993 Gore also debated the North American Free Trade Agreement with H. Ross Perot on *Larry King Live*. He did so well that Congress eventually passed this bill. It was claimed that Gore never asked Clinton's permission before agreeing to the debate, which would show a whole new level of independence for vice presidents (if the claim were proven to be true).

In foreign affairs, Gore attended very few funerals, but he completed a top-secret deal with Russia to bring bomb-grade uranium to the United States.

At home, Gore was consulted on cabinet appointments and kept Clinton from postponing important decisions. Throughout his two terms, Gore maintained a deadpan expression much of the time. Aides to the vice president said that when he discussed Clinton's policies, the only way to tell what Gore thought of them was to watch his eyebrows.

But Gore will probably be best remembered for championing the environment. Among the many problems he fought against were the dumping of hazardous waste, the destruction of the rain forests, and global warming.

The vice presidency has come a long way since the office first came into existence. Although the person in this office will never have more power than the president wishes to share, it is increasingly less likely that vice presidents will ever again be just "presidents in waiting."

Glossary

Amendment—An addition to the body of the Constitution that must be passed by the Senate and the House of Representatives and ratified by all the states to become law.

Balancing the ticket—Picking candidates to run together whose different backgrounds will appeal to different groups.

Cabinet—The president's group of top advisors who are also heads of executive departments. These include the secretary of state, secretary of the treasury, defense secretary, etc.

Caucus—A meeting of individuals who are all from the same political party.

Congress—Body that includes both the Senate and the House of Representatives.

Electoral college—The group of state representatives who actually elect the president and vice president.

Impeach—To put a president or other official on trial for a crime.

Insider—A presidential candidate who has served in the Senate or is otherwise part of the established political or power structure.

Lame duck—An officeholder who is serving out his term and who cannot be or has not been reelected.

Nominee—Someone who has been picked by his party to run for an office.

Outsider—A presidential candidate who is not part of the established power structure.

Precedent—Something done or said that serves as an example to those who follow.

Preside—To serve as the chair of a meeting.

Running mate—A partner in a pair of candidates running for office.

Ticket—A list of candidates put together by a political party.

Further Reading

Feinberg, Barbara Silberdick. *Next in Line.* Danbury, CT: Franklin Watts, 1996.

Hoopes, Roy. *The Changing Vice Presidency.* New York: Thomas Y. Crowell, 1981.

Jeffrey, Laura S. *Al Gore: Leader for a Millennium.* Springfield, NJ: Enslow Publishers, 1999.

Kincade, Vance R. *Heirs Apparent: Solving the Vice Presidential Dilemma.* Westport, CT: Greenwood Publishing Group, 2000.

Pious, Richard M. *The Young Oxford Companion to the Presidency of the United States.* New York: Oxford, 1994.

Walch, Timothy. *At the President's Side.* Columbia, MO: University of Missouri, 1997.

ABOUT THE AUTHOR: Marilyn D. Anderson was born and raised on a dairy farm in Hubert Humphrey's home state. She taught music for seven years in the state where Calvin Coolidge's father lived. Later she moved to Dan Quayle's home state and wrote 16 children's novels, including *Come Home Barkley* and *The Bubble Gum Monster*. She has also written a horse care book for Willowisp Press and a biography of Chris Farley for Chelsea House.

SENIOR CONSULTING EDITOR Arthur M. Schlesinger, jr. is the leading American historian of our time. He won the Pulitzer Prize for his book *The Age of Jackson* (1945) and again for *A Thousand Days* (1965). This chronicle of the Kennedy Administration also won a National Book Award. Professor Schlesinger is the Albert Schweitzer Professor of the Humanities at the City University of New York, and he has been involved in several other Chelsea House projects, including the REVOLUTIONARY WAR LEADERS and COLONIAL LEADERS series.

Picture Credits